THE WORST MAN-MADE ENVIRONMENTAL DISASTERS

Science Book for Kids 9-12
Children's Science & Nature Books

Speedy Publishing LLC
40 E. Main St. #1156
Newark, DE 19711
www.speedypublishing.com
Copyright 2017

All Rights reserved. No part of this book may be reproduced or used in any way or form or by any means whether electronic or mechanical, this means that you cannot record or photocopy any material ideas or tips that are provided in this book.

Our world is a complex, balanced system in which things generally go as they should. When they go wrong, it is often people who have caused the problem. Let's look at the worst human-created environmental disasters.

NATURAL AND UNNATURAL DISASTERS

Because the Earth is a dynamic system, sometimes there can be sudden, violent changes: an earthquake, floods, a fire destroying thousands of acres of forest. The Earth's system is designed to absorb these shocks and rebound from them.

A WILDFIRE BURNS IN A FOREST.

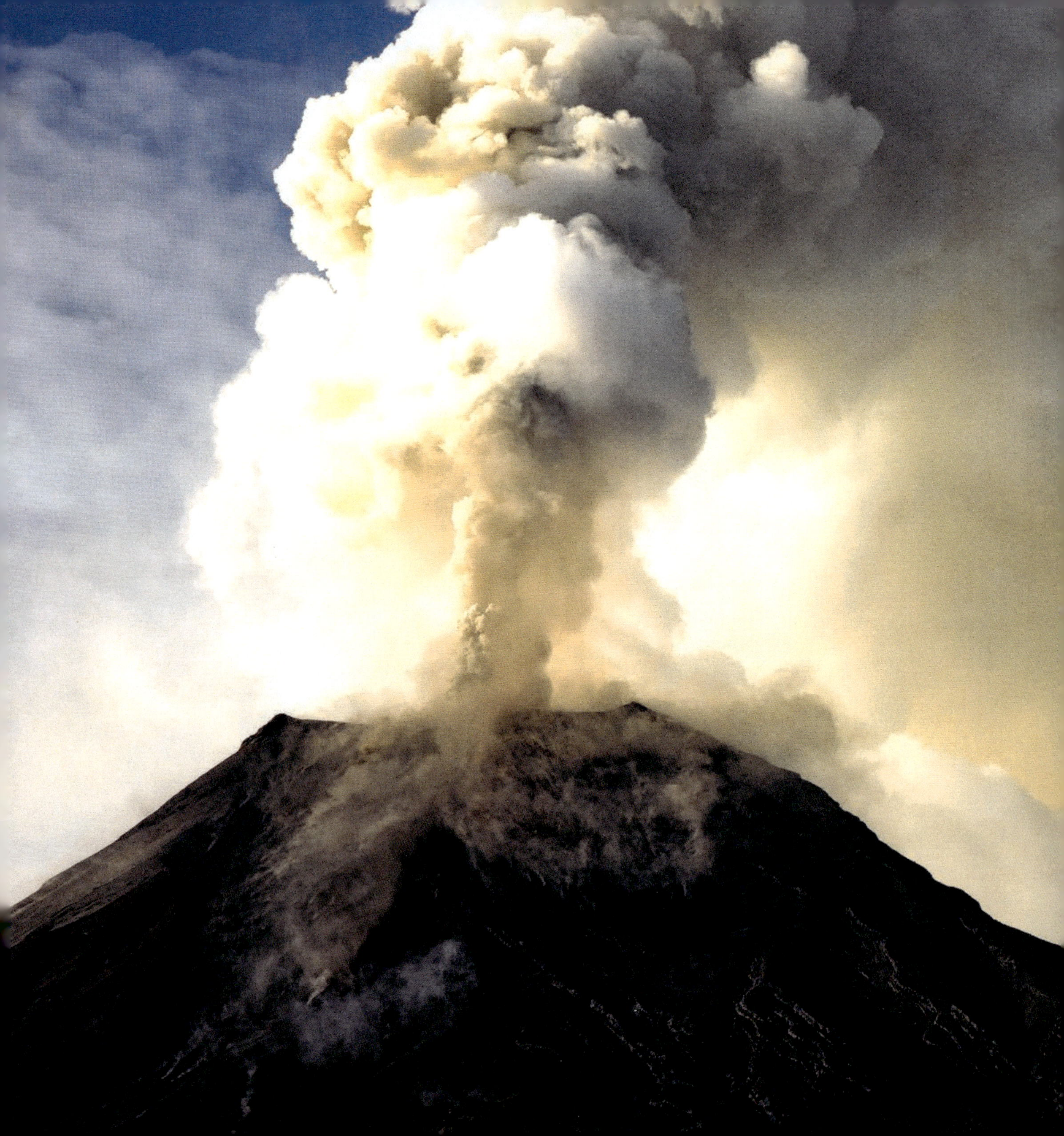

A volcanic eruption can knock down forests and bury the land in ash and lava. But a few decades later that land, enriched by what the volcano spewed out, will support life of all sorts.

VOLCANO ERUPTION

The Earth is finding it harder to absorb and recover from environmental shocks caused by human activity. As we fill the Earth, we are irresponsibly filling it with our junk, chemicals, and other dangerous substances. Read on and learn about some of the worst environmental disasters humans have caused.

MOUNTAINS OF GARBAGE

AIR POLLUTION BY SMOKE COMING OUT OF TWO FACTORY CHIMNEYS.

AIR POLLUTION

LONDON, UK, 1952

As England moved into the Industrial Age, starting in the eighteenth century, the air gradually got less clean. Smoke from coal fires, from foundries, and from other processes made it so city dwellers had to get used to foggy air that was hard to breathe.

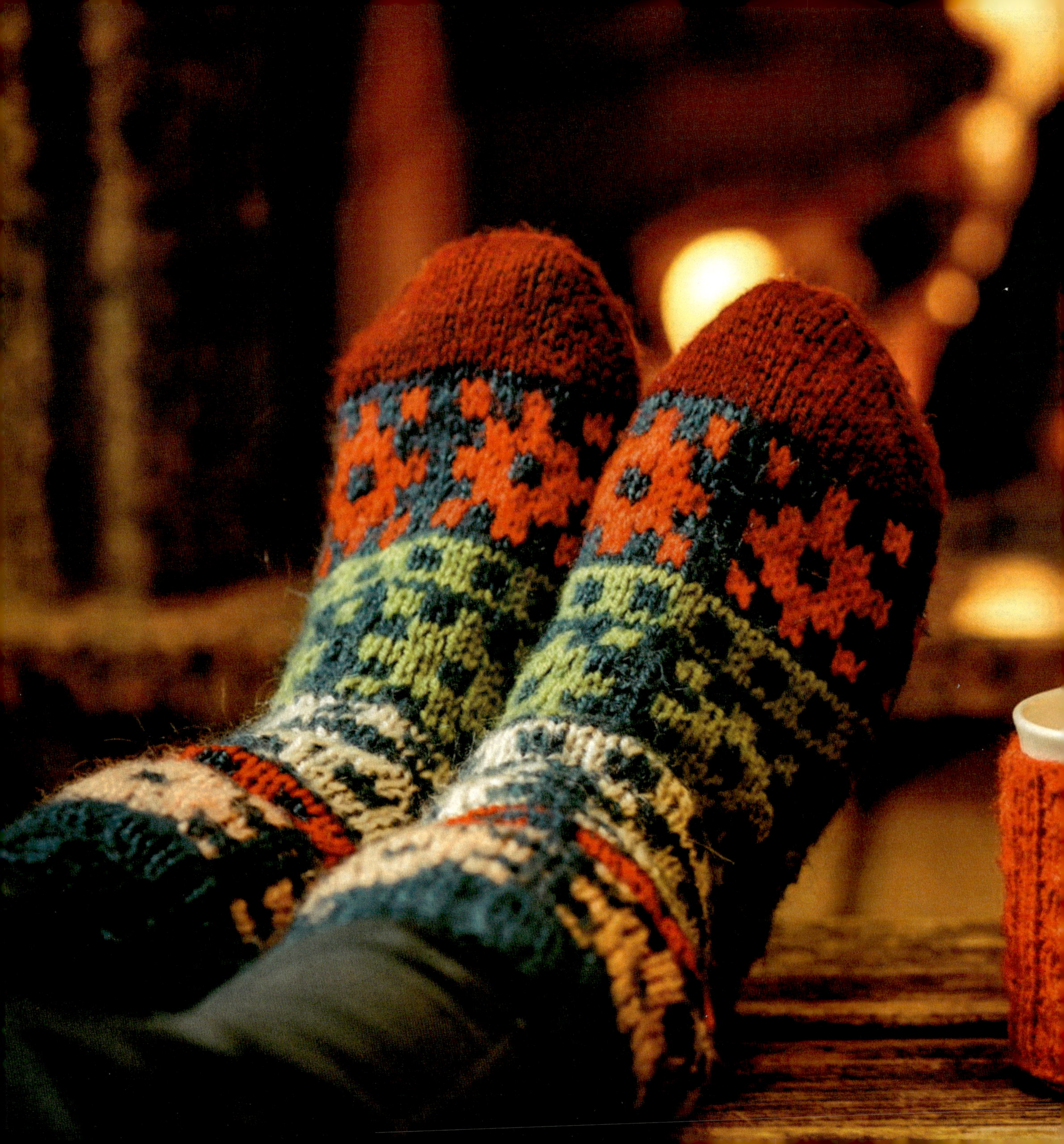

The winter of 1952 was cold and damp, and people burned a lot more coal to heat their houses. The power authority burned more coal to create electricity.

A period of cold air and windless days allowed a thick cloud of smog to form over London. It was so thick that it made the days as dark as night: it was hard to drive, or even to walk, safely. The air was hard to breathe, and over 12,000 people died from breathing-related problems during five long days.

LONDON'S POLLUTED SKYLINE

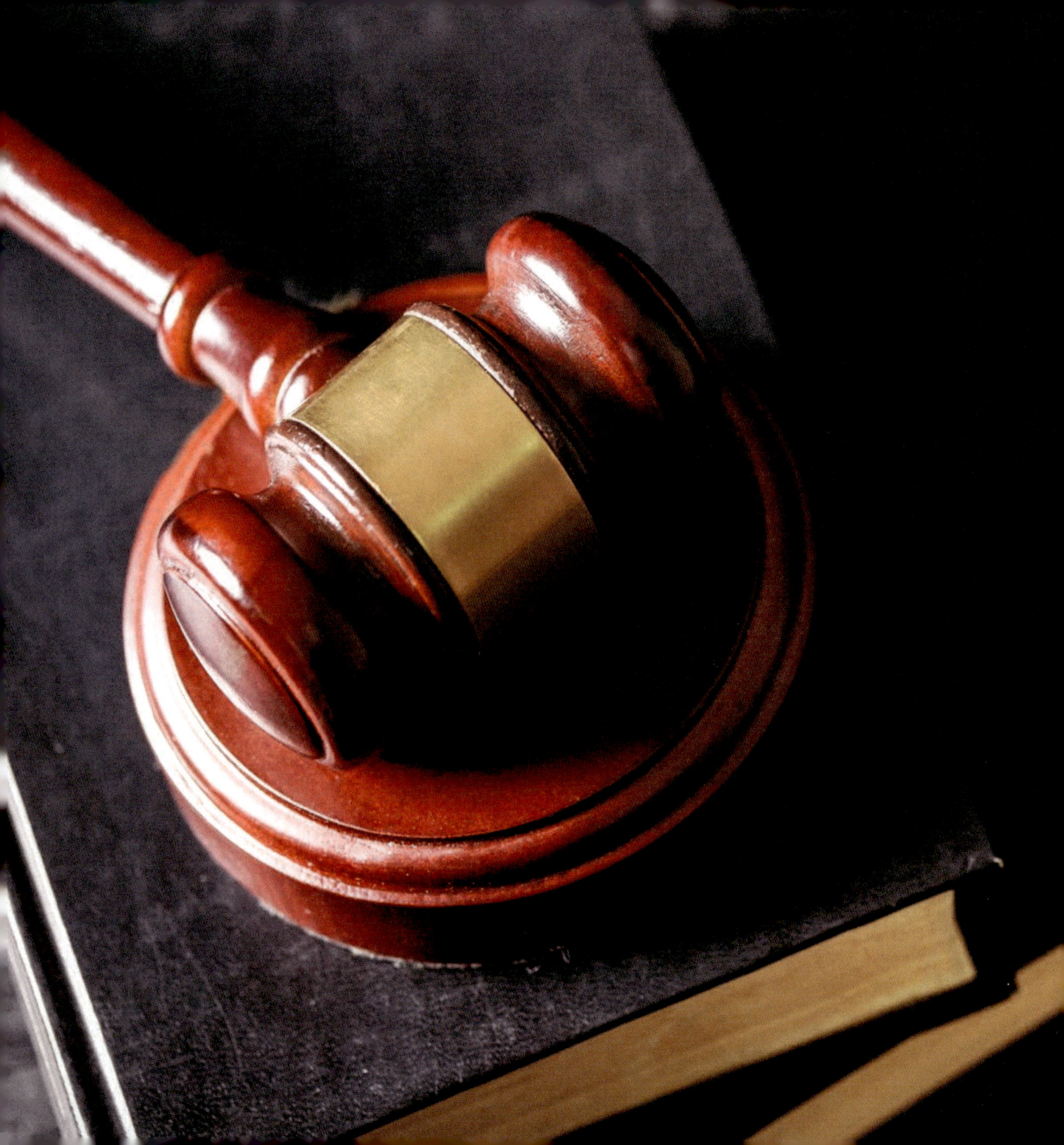

The one positive thing is that the disaster led the government to start making laws to keep the air breathable.

MEDA, ITALY, 1976

In July of 1976, a reactor in a chemical plant in Meda, Italy exploded. The explosion sent a poisonous cloud of dioxin into the air. Nobody died from this accident, but many children came down with a severe skin disease, chloracne, as a result of contact with dioxin.

BOY IN BED WITH SKIN DISEASE

TREES IN THE MOUNTAINS DESTROYED BY ACID RAIN.

FIRES

IRAQ, 2003

Someone started a fire at a sulfur plant in Iraq in June, 2003. The fire burned for a month and sent tons of sulfur dioxide into the air. Sulfur dioxide can increase acid rain, which hurts crops, and can kill people who try to breathe it.

TURKMENISTAN, 1971

Scientists were drilling into the Earth near Derweze, Turkmenistan in 1971. The drill struck a natural reservoir of methane gas, which humans cannot breathe and which is highly flammable. The scientists decided to burn off the gas. They made a huge error in thinking they knew how much gas was in the reservoir. The fire is continuing today!

BLACK SMOKE FROM BURNING OF GAS

HUGE SMOKE CLOUDS AFTER EXPLOSION

KUWAIT, 1991

Iraq invaded Kuwait in 1990. In 1991 a group of countries led by the United States forced the Iraqi Army to retreat. As they moved back, the Iraqis set fire to over 600 oil wells, mainly to prevent the advancing troops from being able to use the oil. The fires burned for almost a year. Huge clouds of black smoke polluted the air of Kuwait and other countries, and it cost over $1.5 billion to put the fires out.

RADIATION

Learn more about the worst nuclear accidents of all time in the Baby Professor book Devastating Nuclear Accidents throughout History: Causes and Results.

THE RADIATION ICON

CHERNOBYL NUCLEAR POWER PLANT

CHERNOBYL, 1986

In April, 1986, workers made a mistake at the nuclear power plant at Chernobyl, in what is now the Ukraine. The release of radiation and radioactive material has made it impossible to live near the site of the plant for the next two hundred years! Many who fought to prevent a nuclear meltdown died as a result of exposure, and there may be as many as one hundred thousand additional cancer deaths in the coming years by people exposed to Chernobyl's radioactive cloud.

THREE MILE ISLAND, 1979

In Pennsylvania in the United States, human error caused a partial core meltdown in a nuclear reactor near Harrisburg. Fortunately the meltdown was contained, but many people have been affected. The rates of premature deaths, miscarriages, and cancers are much higher in the area than they had been.

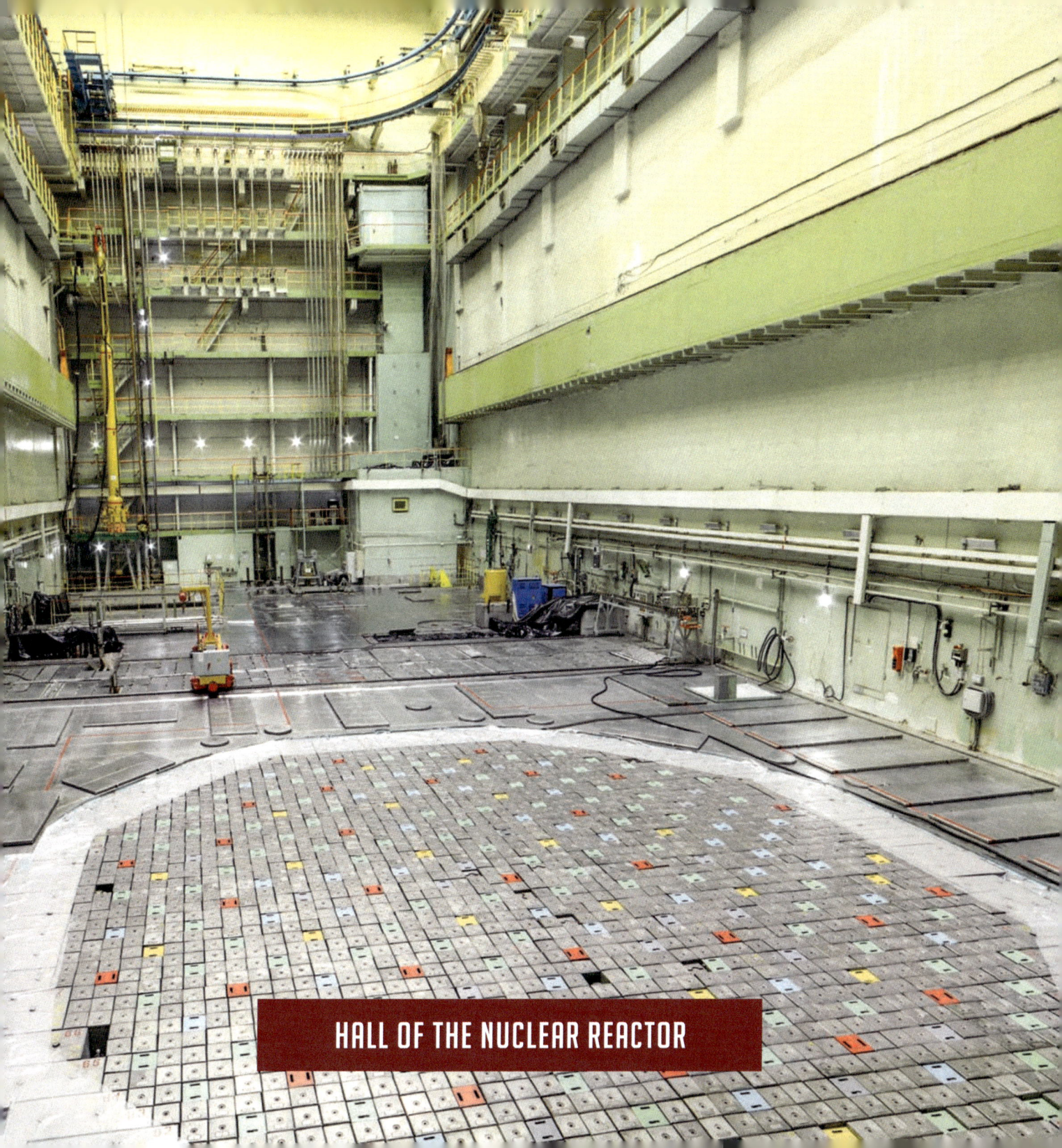

HALL OF THE NUCLEAR REACTOR

BIKINI ATOLL

CASTLE BRAVO

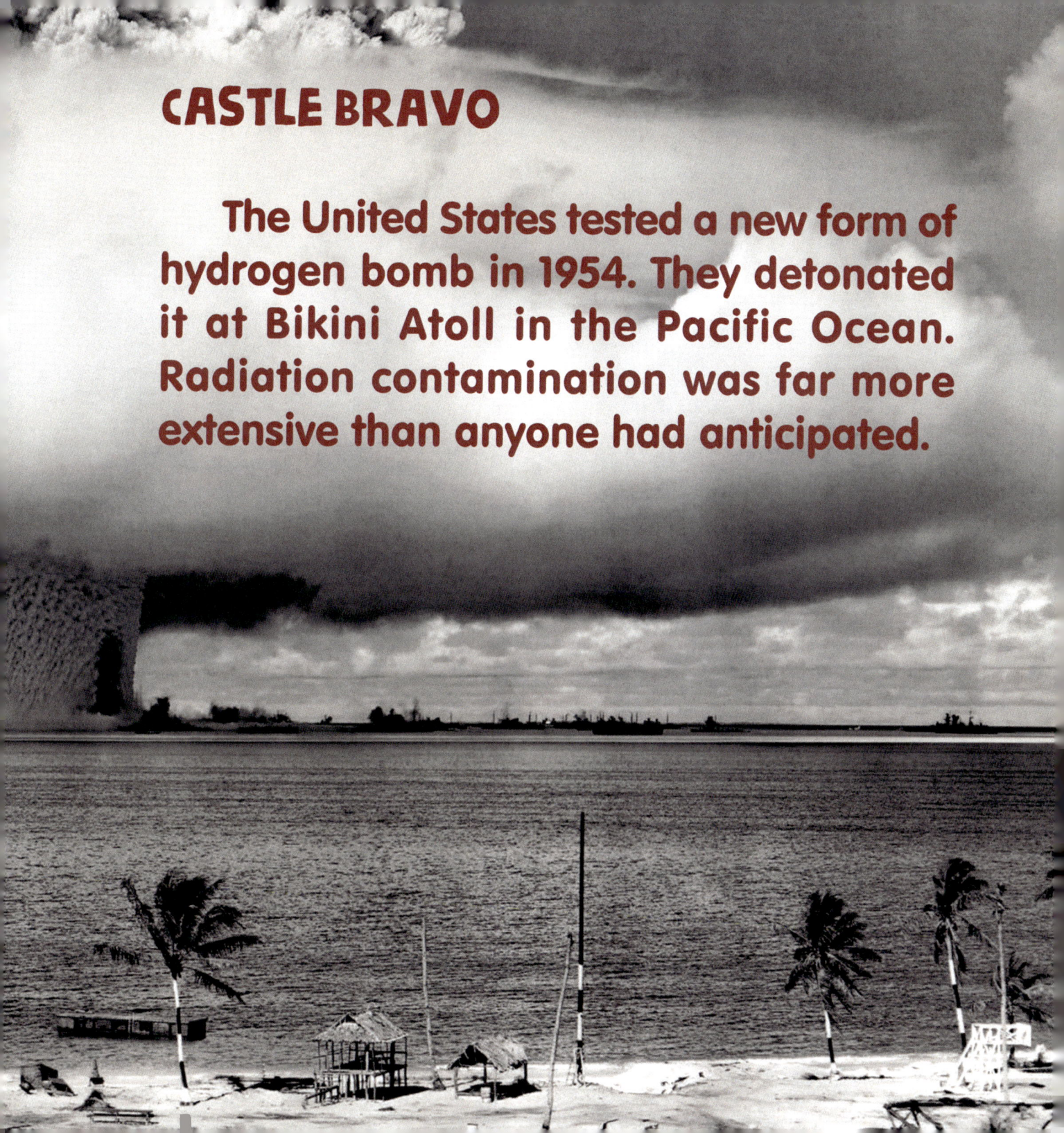

The United States tested a new form of hydrogen bomb in 1954. They detonated it at Bikini Atoll in the Pacific Ocean. Radiation contamination was far more extensive than anyone had anticipated.

CHEMICALS

LOVE CANAL, 1940S TO THE PRESENT

In the community around the Love Canal, near Niagara Falls, New York, people began noticing bad smells and odd puddles of material in their yards. People began getting sick, and babies were born with birth defects.

DIRTY CANAL

TOXIC WASTE

It turned out that the neighborhood had been built over a site where a local chemical company had buried 21,000 tons of toxic waste. The company was trying to save money by just burying the material rather than disposing of it properly. People today continue to suffer the results of their actions.

BHOPAL, 1984

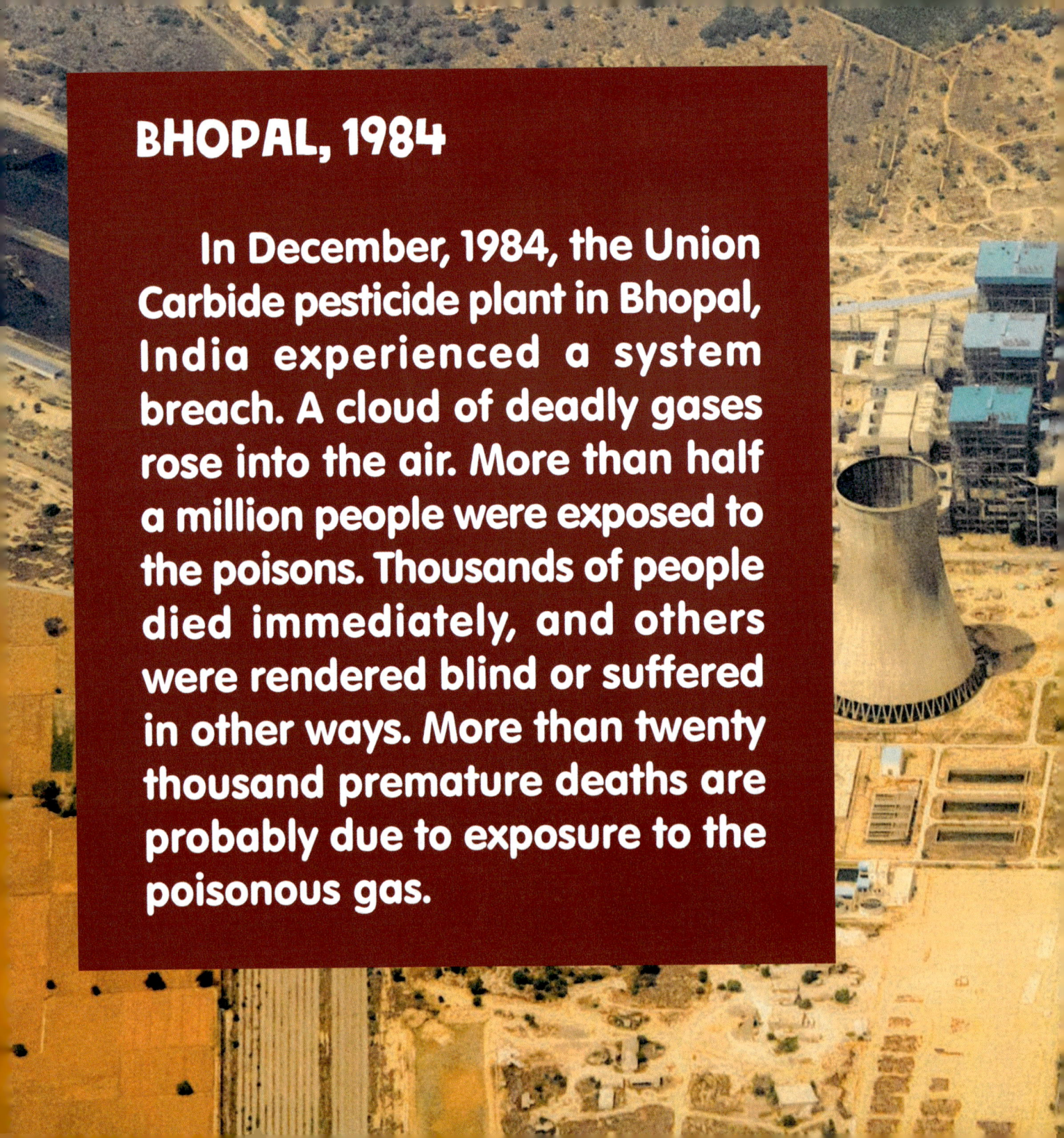

In December, 1984, the Union Carbide pesticide plant in Bhopal, India experienced a system breach. A cloud of deadly gases rose into the air. More than half a million people were exposed to the poisons. Thousands of people died immediately, and others were rendered blind or suffered in other ways. More than twenty thousand premature deaths are probably due to exposure to the poisonous gas.

INDIAN POWERPLANT

BEAUTIFUL GIRL FIGHTING CANCER

JILIN, 2005

A chemical plant in Jilin City, China exploded in November, 2005. Six workers died and dozens more were injured. Tens of thousands of city residents had to flee their homes. Material from the explosion added over 100 tons of pollutants to the Songhua River. This has increased the rate of leukemia among people who use the water for fishing, for drinking, and for other purposes.

MINAMATA, 1956

In 1956, a Japanese chemical company released huge amounts of waste water containing mercury into Minamata Bay. Mercury damages the human nervous system. Over two thousand people died as a result of this pollution.

A SMALL GLASS CONTAINER CONTAINING MERCURY

OIL SPILL

OIL

EXXON VALDEZ, 1989

In March, 1989, an oil tanker hit a reef off the coast of Alaska. Over eleven million gallons of oil spilled into Prince William Sound, polluting over five hundred miles of coast. More than 250,000 birds died as a result of the spill, and unknown numbers of fish and other animals.

DEEP WATER HORIZON, 2010

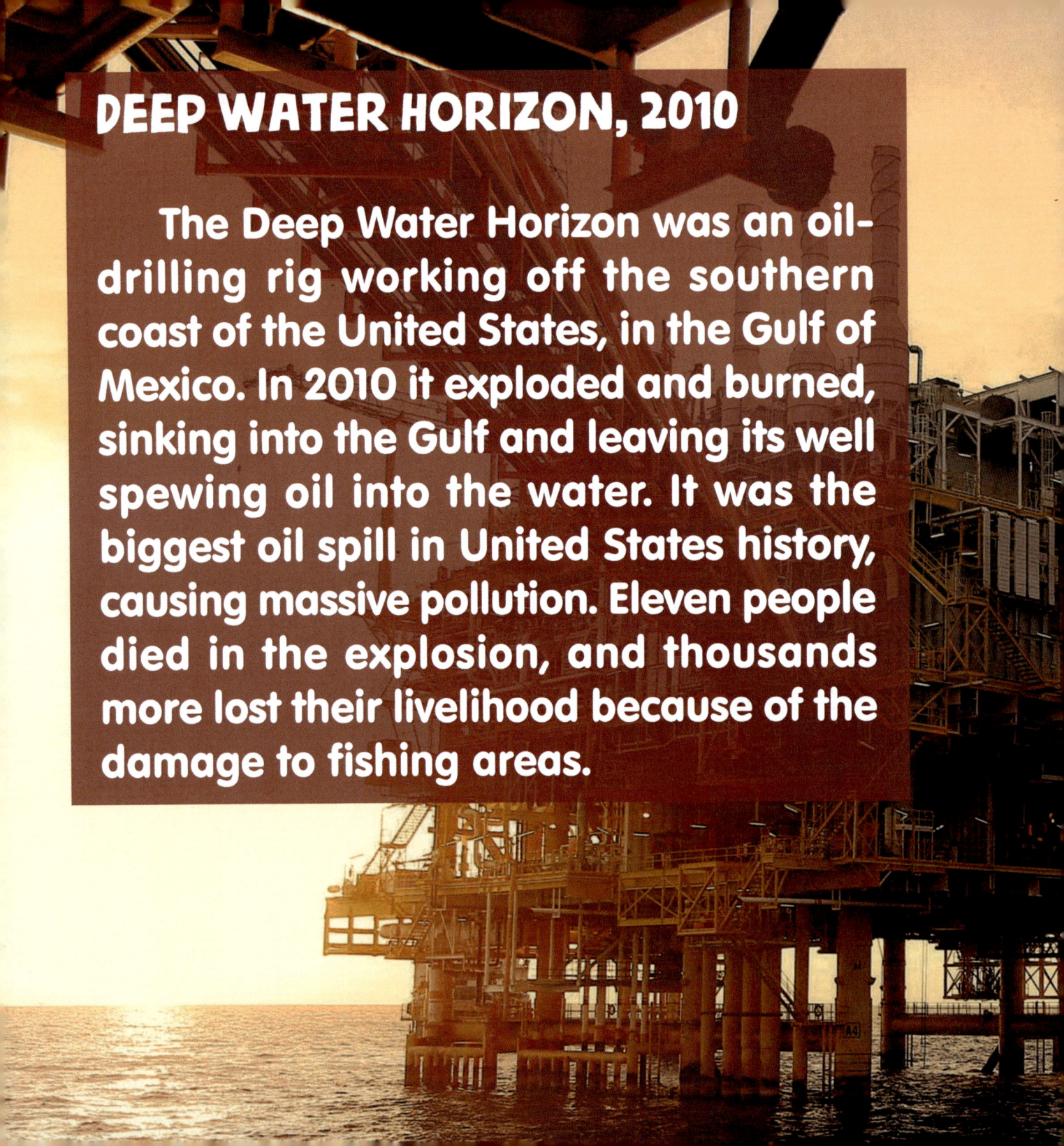

The Deep Water Horizon was an oil-drilling rig working off the southern coast of the United States, in the Gulf of Mexico. In 2010 it exploded and burned, sinking into the Gulf and leaving its well spewing oil into the water. It was the biggest oil spill in United States history, causing massive pollution. Eleven people died in the explosion, and thousands more lost their livelihood because of the damage to fishing areas.

OIL-DRILLING RIG

OTHER ISSUES

GULF OF MEXICO DEAD ZONE

Farmers use a lot of fertilizers on their fields. The fertilizers have chemicals that help plants grow, but that are not good for fish or for the marine environment. A lot of the fertilizer in the United States gets washed into the river systems by rain, and a lot of that gets delivered by the Mississippi River into the Gulf of Mexico.

PLANT WITH FERTILIZER

FISH DIE DUE TO WATER POLLUTION

This has created a "dead zone" where the levels of nitrogen, phosphorus and other nutrients mean that fish can no longer survive there.

THE ARAL SEA

The Aral Sea in Russia used to be one of the four largest freshwater lakes in the world. In the 1960s the government of the Soviet Union started diverting the waters flowing into the Aral Sea for use in irrigation projects. So much water has been diverted that the Aral Sea is now just ten percent of its natural size. This has devastated plant and animal life for hundreds of miles around.

OLD SHIP AT THE SHORE OF ARAL SEA, UZBEKISTAN

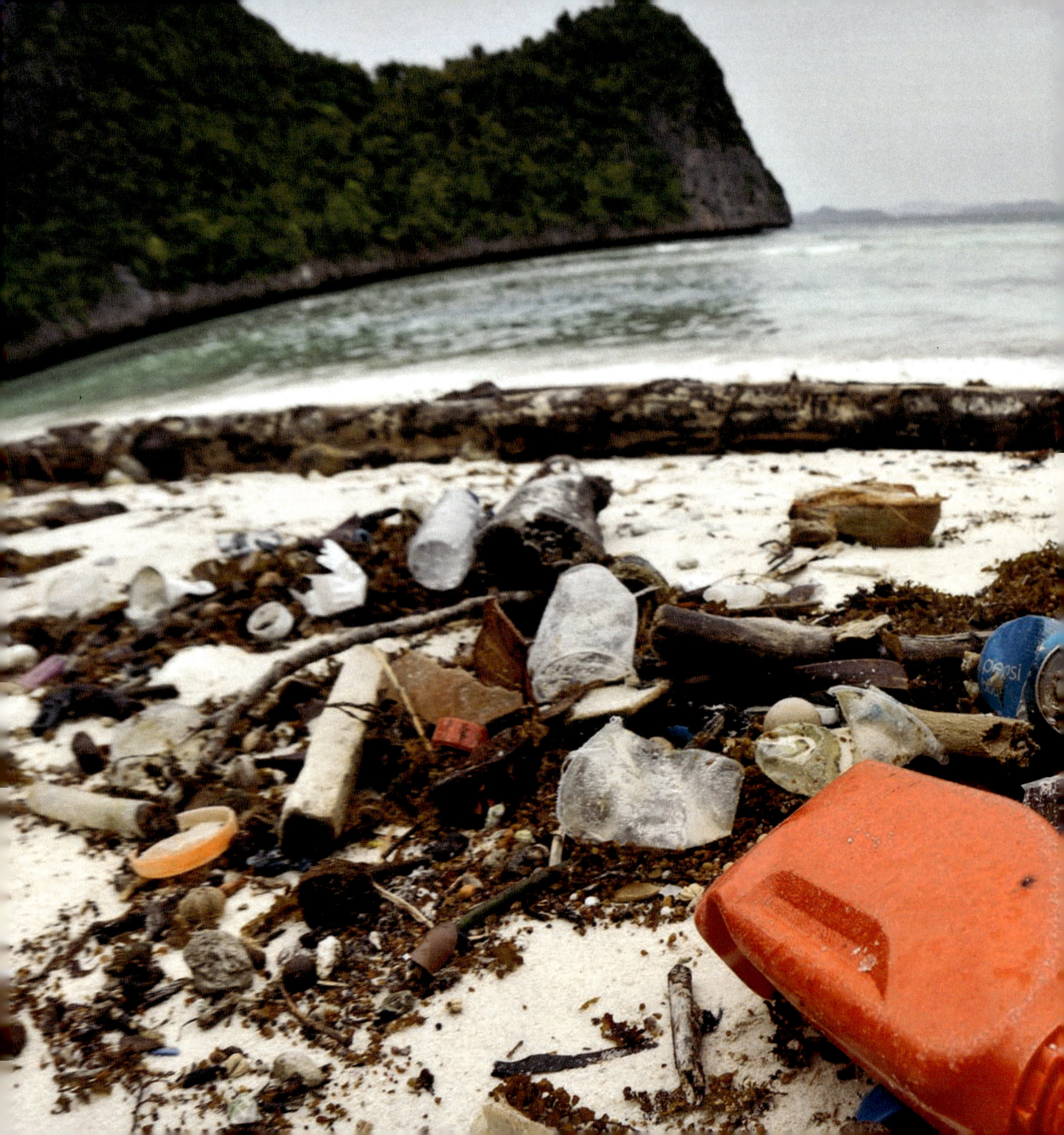
pepsi

THE PACIFIC GYRE GARBAGE PATCH

There is a huge layer of plastic floating in the Pacific Ocean, formed of chemical sludge and garbage in every form, from soft-drink bottles to discarded insulation. This soup of plastic waste now covers over 400,000 square miles. The plastic is slowly breaking down into toxic chemicals and micro-beads that fish can eat. Both the fish, and any other creature that later eats the fish, suffer from ingesting the plastic chemicals.

E-WASTE

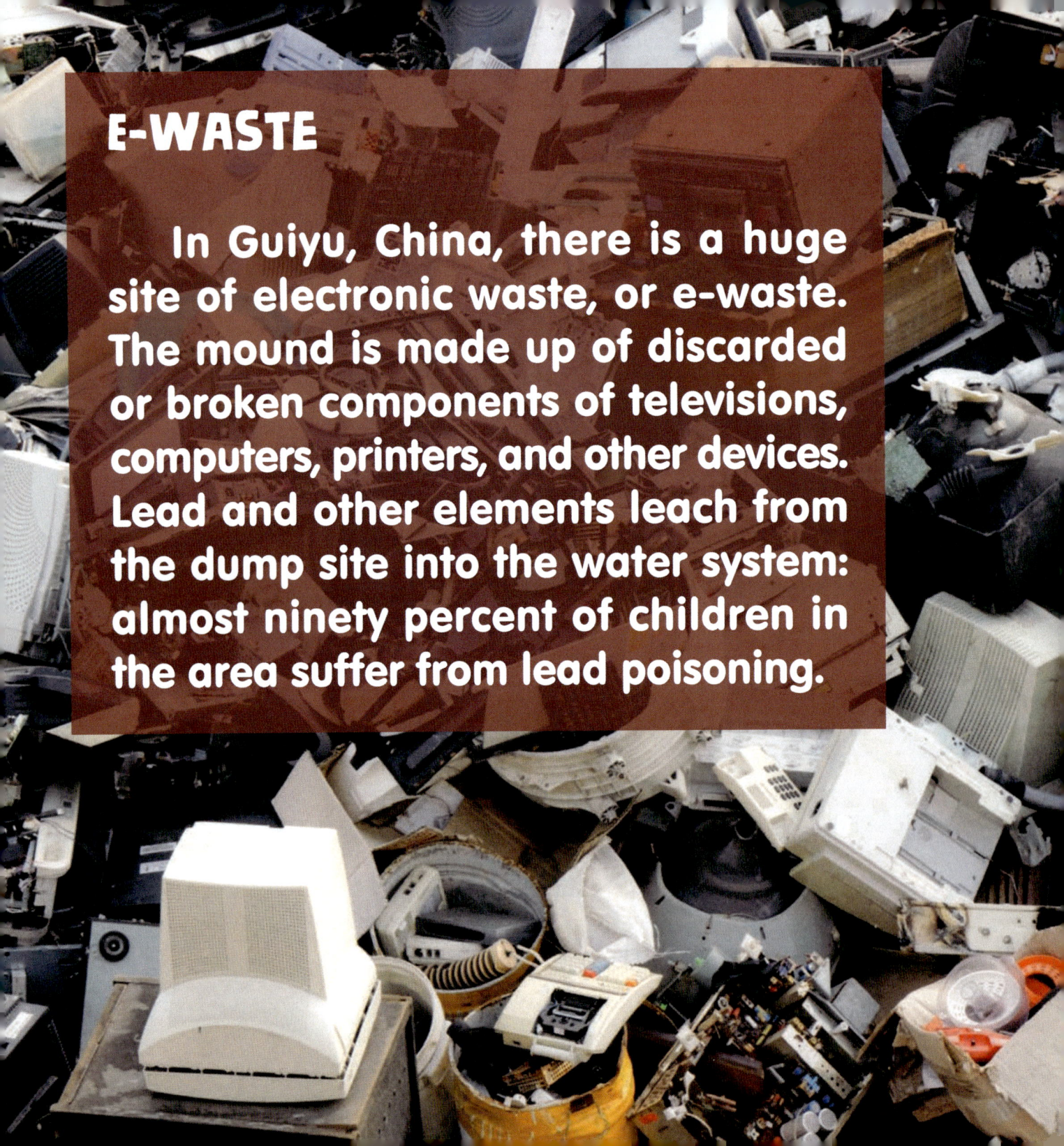

In Guiyu, China, there is a huge site of electronic waste, or e-waste. The mound is made up of discarded or broken components of televisions, computers, printers, and other devices. Lead and other elements leach from the dump site into the water system: almost ninety percent of children in the area suffer from lead poisoning.

ELECTRONIC WASTE

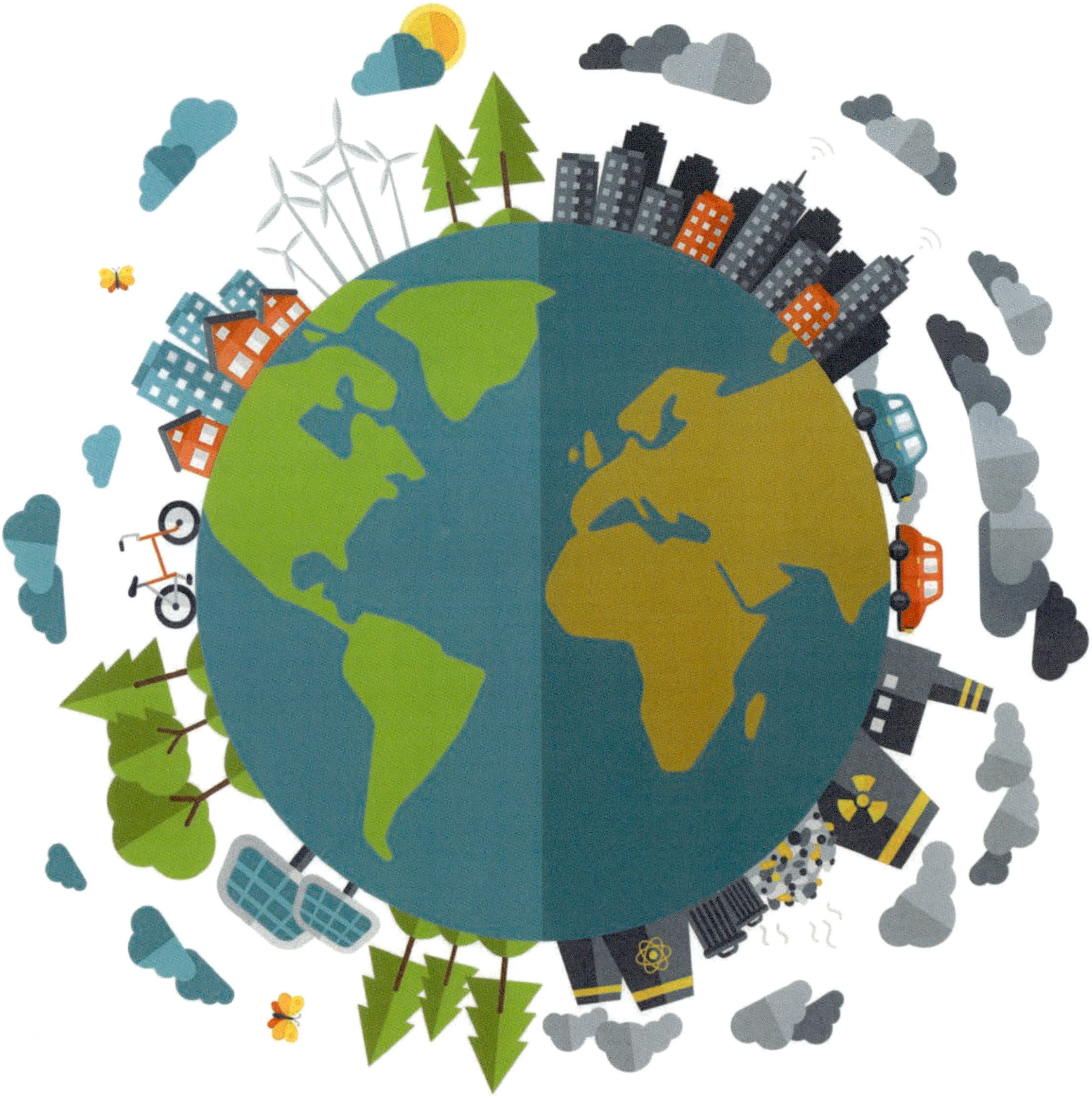

HOW MUCH CAN THE EARTH ABSORB?

Humans are a part of the Earth's ecosystem, but we have grown so numerous and so powerful that now we can create disruptions that it is hard for the Earth to recover from. We act as if we can dump endless junk into a river, and the river will carry it away without being changed; but that is no longer the case. We are reaching the limits of how flexible our ecosystem can be.

Extreme weather and climate change are signs that human actions are causing extreme reactions in Earth's systems. Read more about this in the Baby Professor books Mother Earth Needs a Band-aid! and Pollution: Problems Made by Man.

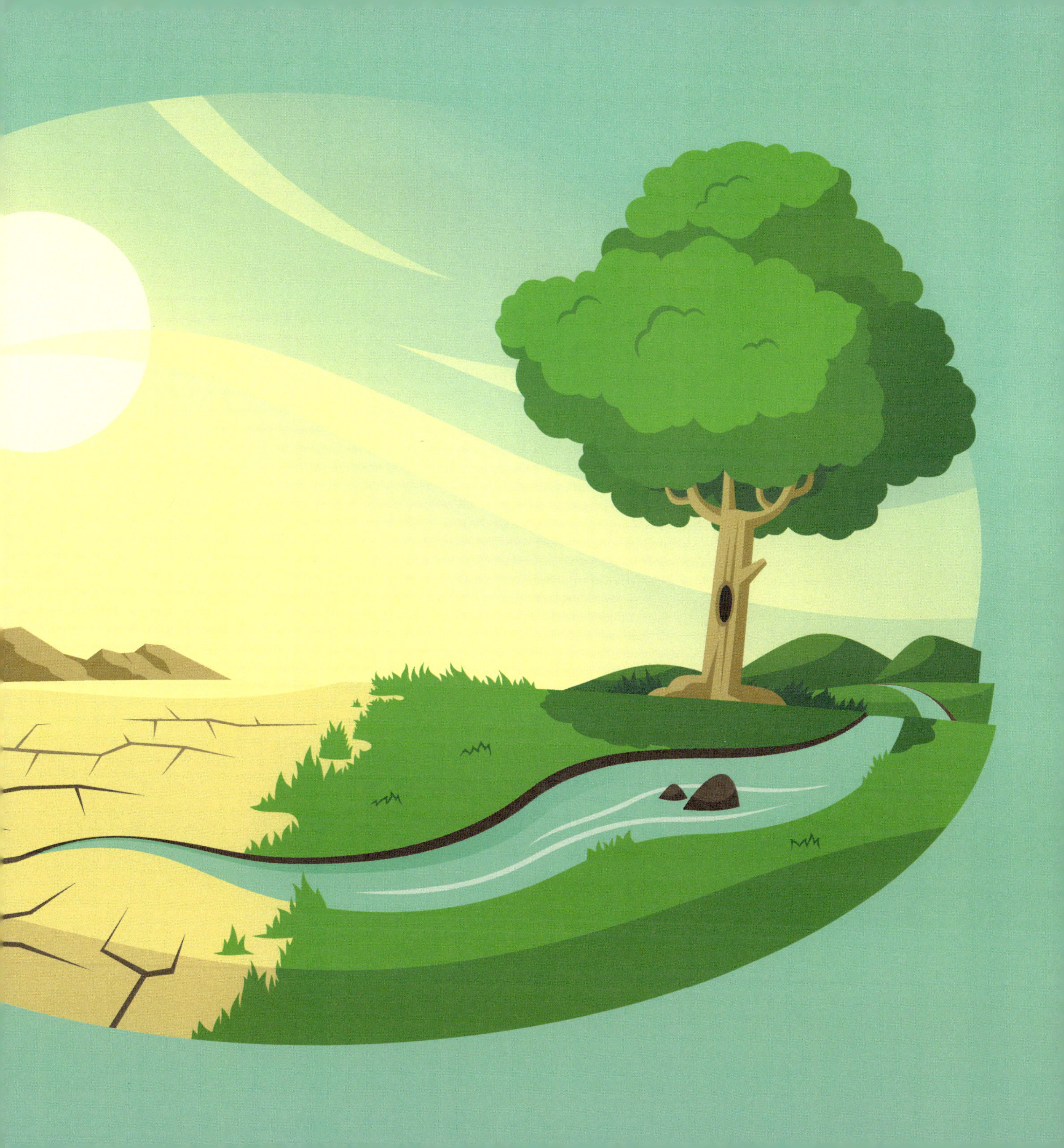

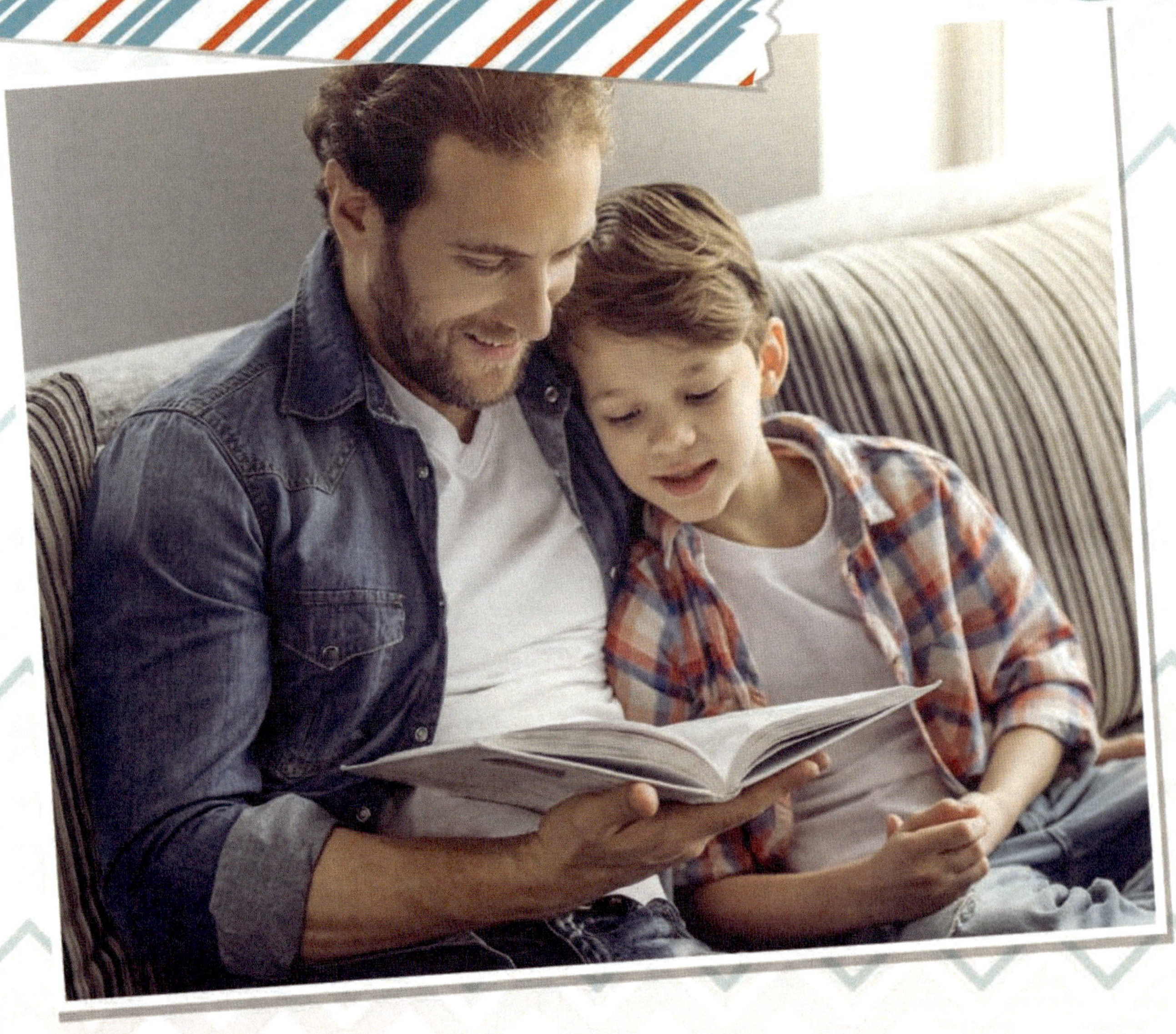

Visit

BABY PROFESSOR
EDUCATION KIDS

www.BabyProfessorBooks.com

to download Free Baby Professor eBooks and view
our catalog of new and exciting Children's Books

Made in the USA
Middletown, DE
27 August 2019